VERSES for DAD'S HEART

Verses *for* Dad's Heart

By Steven L. Layne

Illustrations by Gail Greaves Klinger

PELICAN PUBLISHING COMPANY

Gretna 2004

In memory of Richard L. Layne, Lindal Brown, and
Jim Ferguson: Good Men . . . Great Fathers. And with love
to Charles E. Dover, for being my second father
right from the start.—SLL

To the unconditional love of our heavenly Father, and to the legacy
of godly men like my dad, Harold Greaves.—GGK

Author and Illustrator's Special Tribute:
With gratitude to Dr. James Dobson,
for serving as a much-needed
"father figure" to so many of America's families.

The word "Pelican" and the depiction of a pelican are trademarks
of Pelican Publishing Company, Inc., and are registered
in the U.S. Patent and Trademark Office.

Library of Congress Cataloging-in-Publication Data

Layne, Steven L.
   Verses for dad's heart / by Steven L. Layne ; illustrated by Gail
Greaves Klinger.
     p. cm.
   ISBN 1-58980-145-8 (hardcover : alk. paper)
 1. Fathers—Poetry. 2. Father and child—Poetry. I. Title.
    PS3612.A96 V47 2004
    811'.54—dc22

                            2003018908

Printed in China

Published by Pelican Publishing Company, Inc.
1000 Burmaster Street, Gretna, Louisiana 70053

Superheroes

Superheroes don't wear capes;
They wear sweatshirts,
With someone's favorite sports team's logo on them.
(The sweatshirts come in both adult and child sizes.)

Superheroes don't see through solid objects;
They see into the heart
Of someone who was made fun of at school.
(The heart just *might* get repaired over a Mambo Brownie Delight.)

Superheroes aren't faster than a speeding bullet;
They are slow and patient,
Especially when someone is trying something for the first time.
(Who realizes the value of training wheels until they're gone?)

Superheroes don't protect everyone from everything;
They let someone experience the consequences
Of very poor decisions.
(The detention room is *not* a good place to make friends.)

Superheroes *are* more powerful than a locomotive,
If the love they have for others . . .

Is anything at all
Like the love my dad has for me.

Daddy Never Fails

Reading silly stories
Chasing me around
Singing made-up nonsense songs
Falling on the ground

Giving me a bottle
Tossing me a ball
Playing with my bathtub toys
Running if I call

Rocking me at bedtime
Telling me some tales
Holding me when things aren't right . . .

Daddy never fails

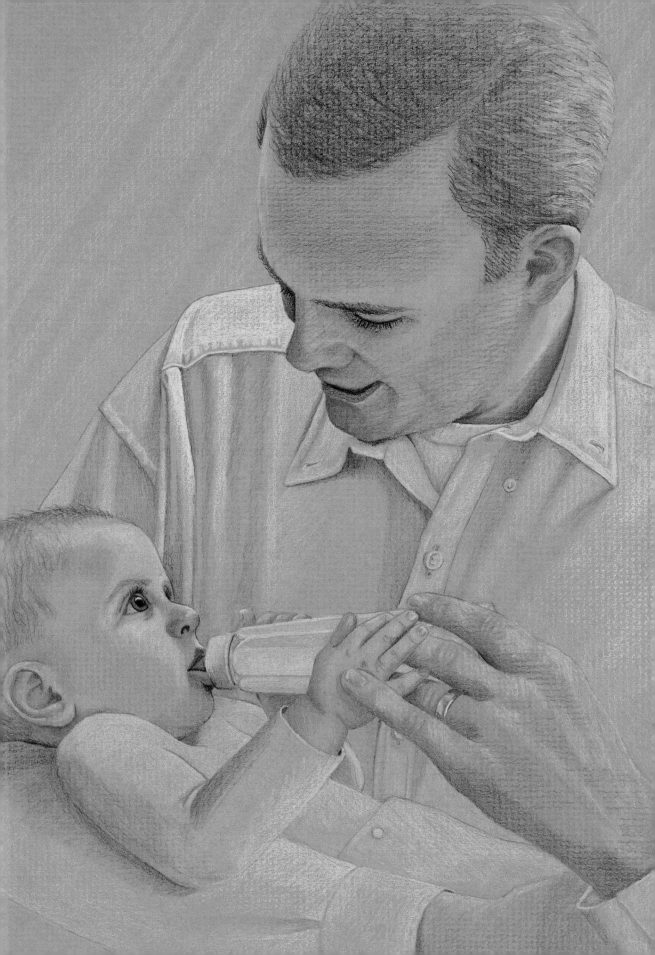

You'll Do

I got this dump truck, see,
And I need someone to sit over there
And roll it back and forth with me
And look really, really interested
. . . You'll do.

I got this new racetrack, see,
And the cover of the box shows the ninety-two pieces
Fitting together perfectly so that my little cars will really *go!*
And I need someone to help me build it
. . . You'll do.

I got this book called *Brown Bear, Brown Bear,* see,
And just after Mom read it to me for the 132nd time, it got misplaced
And I've torn the house apart looking for it, but—no luck!
And I need someone to help me retrieve this lost literary treasure
. . . You'll do.

As I stop to consider the difficulties I encounter
As a part of my day-to-day experiences at the age of two,
It strikes me, Dad, that *you'll do* quite nicely
As the solution for all of them.

My Daddy

My daddy
Is a very, very, very good man.

He reads the very best books
And sings the very best songs.

He tells the very best jokes.
And rights the very worst wrongs.

My daddy
Is a very, very, very good man.

Mr. Fix-It

Dad's not so good with hammers;
He's not the best with saws.
With doors that creak or pipes that leak
He's really a lost cause.

He's scary with a power drill;
With nuts and bolts he's bad!
But when my *heart* needs big repairs,
There's no one like my dad.

On the Job

Billy says *his* dad's an architect.
He draws houses and churches and big corporate buildings
for all kinds of important people.

Sally says *her* dad's a doctor.
He gives shots, writes prescriptions, and helps people
with all kinds of important diseases.

Tom and Nancy say *their* dad's a lawyer.
He meets with clients, persuades juries, and convinces judges
on all kinds of important matters.

But, you know, Dad,
I like what you do best of all.
What you do is *very* important—ultra-important! That's what I told them.

In fact, I said that if you didn't keep on doing what you do,
This world would be in a *whole lot of trouble*, Dad.

Dad . . .
What is it that you do, again?

Who Dad Used to Be

It's fun to hear stories
About who Dad used to be.
It's hard to think he had a life
Before my folks had me.

Dad used to be a sales guy.
He used to raise Great Danes.
He used to stay up late at night and play real silly games.

He used to climb big mountains.
He used to dance a lot.
He used to speed on boulevards and *never once* got caught.

He used to play the saxophone.
He used to travel far.
He used to serve the National Guard and study CPR.

It's fun to hear stories
About who Dad used to be.
But the man my dad is here and now's the best.
He's *Dad . . .* to me!

Thanks for Loving Mom

Thanks for loving Mom,
Dad,
The way that you do.

Thanks for letting me see . . .
Your arms around her when Grandma died,
Your lips touching hers after dinnertime prayers,
Your hand joined with one of hers when we take walks as a family.

Thanks for letting me hear . . .
You recite the love poem you wrote for her so many years ago,
You describe how she took your breath away the first time you saw her,
You tell her that you love her at least once a day.

Thanks for letting me know . . .
The memories of her that you savor,
The day-to-day problems that you work through as a couple,
The dreams you both have for your future together.

Thanks for loving Mom,
Dad,
So steadfast and true.

Because the way you love Mom,
Dad,
Helps me feel loved, too.

Dad's Favorite

I've always been Dad's favorite.
I'm sure it must be true.
I see it when he tells me
How he loves me through and through.

I'll always be Dad's favorite.
I tell you it's the truth.
He cheers for me and holds me close.
There is no better proof.

There's just one thing that puzzles me;
I haven't got a clue—
Why all my *siblings* seem to think
That they're his favorites, too.

Some Very Interesting Things about My Dad That I Would Like to Write Down in a Poem

My dad told my mom that every boy should have a dog;
Now, I have a dog.

My dad bought a machine that sprayed sticky stuff on our deck to seal it
    in six easy steps;
Now, the neighbors don't like us, and we pay people to spray sticky stuff
    on our deck.

My dad rode the roller-coaster with me eleven times last Saturday at Six
    Flags;
Now, I know what Pepto-Bismol is.

My dad sent a lot of flowers to my mom for no particular reason;
Now, Mom is humming and smiling a lot,
    but I am still never sending flowers to a girl.

My dad came to school to tell what he does at work all day;
Now, I know what he does at work all day (sort of),
    but I don't want to explain it.

My dad took me to his best pizza place and to see his favorite team;
Now, my dad and I are practically the same because we like all the same
    things.

My dad told my mom that we were not getting a new car;
Now, we have a new minivan, and I have my own cup holder.

My dad showed me the medal my grandpa won in the war;
Now, I understand the Pledge of Allegiance.

My dad gave one of his kidneys to his brother;
Now, my aunt doesn't cry anymore.

My dad gave me a letter he wrote to me before I could even read;
Now, I understand the true nature of love.

I've thought a lot about all the things my dad has done and said;
And I've decided that they make a very good poem—

Just like my dad . . . makes a very good man.

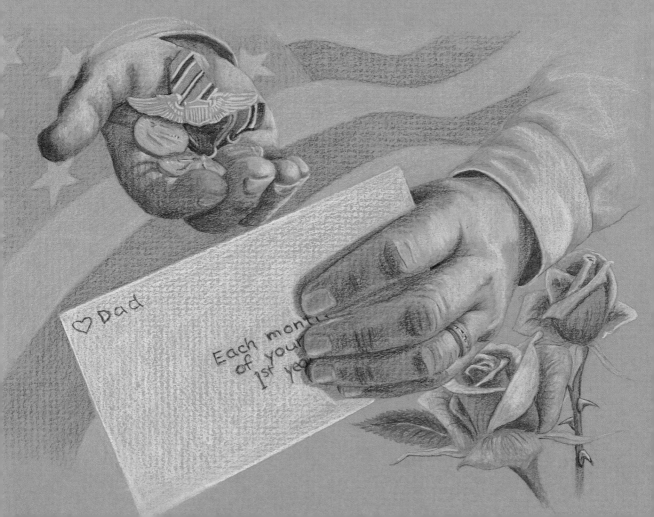

What Matters Most

Mom's off to work
And Dad's staying home.
When some people heard it
They ran for the phone.

Dad and Mom ignore the talk.
They can't abide the fuss.
They keep their eyes upon their goal

That *someone's*
Home with us.

What Is It about Dad?

What is it about Dad always being around
That makes me feel so . . .

Empowered,
Encouraged, and
Edified

Satisfied,
Safe, and
Secure

Maybe it's *just* that . . .
That Dad's always around

Thinking about It Now

Thinking about it now
I know that you were right.

But sometimes deep inside me
I seem to need the fight.

There's so much going on,
It feels like no one understands.

I ask for wise advice
And then I follow my own plans.

I shout for independence.
I demand more privacy.

I say that I don't need you
To support or comfort me.

You've said it's hard to be my age
And, Dad, I think you're right.

So . . .

No matter what my *mouth* might say
My heart says hold on tight.

The Inquisition

You always want to know where I'm going.

You always want to know who I'm with.

You always want to know what I'm doing.

You always want to know when I'll be home.

You always want to know why I feel the way I do.

You sure do ask a lot of questions, Dad.

Thanks.

Remember

Hey, Dad

Remember when I was six
And you helped me set up a lemonade stand outside our house?
You left the office three times that day to buy more lemonade!
You said I was selling the best lemonade in town.

Remember when I was eleven
And we were learning about different holiday customs in school?
You took me to the library, and we did research for three hours!
You came to school when I gave my report for the class.

Remember when I was seventeen
And my best friend's mom was killed by a drunk driver?
You walked up to the casket with me and stayed for the funeral.
You told me that you were hurting with me.

I hope you remember all those times, Dad.

I know that I do.

5¢
Lemonade

The Letter to Dad

Write him a letter,
That's what I ought to do.

I'll tell him
That I'm not his little girl anymore.

That I don't need backrubs or the car keys
And I don't need him to buy me clothes anymore.

I'll tell him
That I have my own job and a brand-new apartment
  now.

That I don't need him looking out for me
And that I don't *want* him checking up on me.

I'll tell him
That I am a progressive, self-sufficient young woman who's doing
  just fine on her own!

That I can't be hampered by parental interference
And that he has to learn to let me make my own mistakes.

Forget the letter.
Now that my phone is working,
I'll just *call* him.

Hi, friends! You've reached the Warren home. Kelly and I decided to be impulsive, and we've gone away on a cruise to Alaska. We're sure you'll all be fine without us. See you when we get back, but leave us a message if you can't wait. Bye!

[*beep*]

"*Daddy!* It's your little *Foo Foo Bear.* . . . I . . . I . . . My phone is working now! Daddy, how could you leave without telling me? What if something happens? What if I *need* you? I hope you're going to be checking your messages. Call me right away on my cell phone so that I'll know how to reach you if there's an emergency. Besides, the light in my bathroom keeps going out, and there's a cracked tile in the kitchen. Oh, and there's this insurance guy who called and said that I should really think about flood insurance. Do I need flood insurance? And it says 'no pets' on that form I signed when I moved in here, but I was thinking about getting a dog because it doesn't seem fair that . . . " [*beep*]

Dad at His Best

Disciplining me when I needed it
And assuring me of your unconditional love afterwards

Showing me how to do something
And then patiently letting me work at it until I got it right

Coming to my games, concerts, and other special events
And never cheering so loudly that I died of embarrassment

Encouraging me in every endeavor that interested me
And offering tangible support to demonstrate your confidence

Giving advice when I asked for it
And keeping quiet when I didn't

Telling me about the mistakes you made
And trusting me to learn the lessons vicariously

Allowing me to experience failure
And helping me learn to deal with it as a part of life

This has been you, Dad—at your best

Someday

Someday—

I sure heard that word a lot.

Someday, you can have your own bicycle.

Someday, boys won't seem so bad.

Someday, you'll be old enough for makeup.

Someday, you'll wish you'd never had that haircut.

Someday, you'll follow your own rules.

Someday, you'll understand why.

Someday, it won't hurt so much.

Someday, you'll see Grandpa again.

Today, Dad,

As I held your granddaughter on my lap

And tried to explain away another of the world's injustices,

I heard your words coming out of my mouth

and I knew.

Someday—it's finally here.

Daddy's Hands

Daddy's hands were warm and tender
When he tucked me in at night.
With a kiss, a hug, a blanket tug,
The world was made all right.

Daddy's hands were strong and steady
On my graduation day.
With a smile and wink, he made me think
Troubled times were far away.

Daddy's hands were soft and fragile
When I came to say goodbye
And I told him of his selfless love,
A gift that would not die.

Many years have passed, and Daddy's gone,
But as I use my hands each day,
To strengthen family ties, I realize . . .
Daddy's never gone away.